TV — Becoming Unglued

Becoming Unglued

A Guide To Help Children Develop Positive TV Habits

WRITTEN BY ADDIE JURS

CARTOONS BY DANA SUMMERS

ROBERT ERDMANN PUBLISHING · SAN MARCOS, CALIFORNIA

Published by Robert Erdmann Publishing
810 W. Los Vallecitos Blvd., #210
San Marcos, CA 92069

Printed in the United States of America
920123456789

Library of Congress Cataloging-in-Publication Data
Jurs, Addie
    TV becoming unglued: a guide to help children develop positive TV habits /
written by Addie Jurs: cartoons by Dana Summers.
        p.   cm.
    Includes bibliographical references and index/
    ISBN 0-945339-25-9: $7.95
    1. Television and children—United States. I. Summers, Dana.
II. Title. III. Title: Television becoming unglued. IV. Title: Becoming unglued.
HQ784.T4J87   1992
302.23'45'083—dc20   92-9315
                                                            CIP
                                                            AC

Dedicated to our sons,
Michael, Stuart, and Douglas,
who continue to teach me all I don't know about parenting.

PREFACE

The magic of television to educate, stimulate and pacify has captured the American home. Many living rooms are now called TV rooms because the TV set is its central focus. But spending endless hours in front of the TV is not the best way for children to live.

Growing and developing children are shaped by each day's life experiences. Children learn most by doing, and then discovering the reaction of their world to their own actions. To do this they must become involved with real people in the real world. Many shows do not communicate the real world; they do not show the real pain a person feels in getting shot, or the real outcomes of sex, or the real life consequences of high speed car chases.

Children need a sense of power and the ability to influence the course of their own lives as well as the experience of affecting the lives of the real people they meet. Each hour they spend passively observing "life" on the TV screen is an hour gone forever. Childhood may seem forever to children, but looking back we know that it goes all too fast.

Children's values are learned. If they spend most of their time watching television, they absorb the values or lack of values they see on the screen. What children see on TV is what television producers let them see. The pictures are usually focused on a small part of life and designed to capture an audience. Sex and violence grab most people's attention, so these are subjects routinely emphasized. Children cannot help but be conditioned by these messages. For them to develop into competent, confident and socially responsible citizens they need to learn about real life and real values from real people.

These are reasons I was so pleased to see Addie Jurs' manuscript develop into a very helpful book for parents. It offers practical ways for families to live comfortably and productively with television. It helps families question the images they see and compare them with their own experiences and values. More importantly, it suggests various effective methods families can use to limit their time in front of the screen.

Addie started with the same practical problem that faces all parents—how to get her children back into real life and unglued from the TV. With her usual enthusiasm, she convinced her husband to develop a convenient device to "put away" the TV. Articles about this solution appeared in *Family Circle, Focus on the Family, Working Mother,* and newspapers throughout the country. Many parents shared their experiences concerning children and TV with Addie. This book combines some of these true stories with her experience and extensive research.

TV—Becoming Unglued can empower your family to take control of the TV. With this guide, TV can become a friend that can enrich you and your child's life.

Glenn Austin, M. D., Pediatrician
Author of *Love and Power/Parent and Child* and
Grandparenting For The 90s.
Former President, The American Academy of Pediatrics.

ACKNOWLEDGMENTS

TV — Becoming Unglued grew from an opportunity nourished with an idea. For the opportunity I thank Lowell Robertson, and for the idea, Mihaly Csikszentmihalyi, Ph.D.

Ideas do not automatically appear cogently on the printed page. I am indebted to my husband Jerry who saved me from sounding ridiculous on more than one occasion. After I first thought I had finished the book, Paul Frommer had the honesty to tell me it was awful. He sent me to the library with a list of books to read. If this book is readable, it's because of him. Marty Travelli made sure I dotted my I's and had the other little marks in place that make English easier to understand.

I am grateful for the abilities of Dana Summers who captures an idea and communicates it with humor in his cartoons. Rebecca Lemna gets the credit for taking all the pieces and putting them together in an appealing package.

Lucky is the writer who has cheerleaders — mine are Leonard Jason, Ph.D., Jan Huskisson, Margaret Winkelmann, Le Von Poquet and Fred and Grace Young. Each has encouraged me and helped me find my direction.

Finally, there are my publisher, Bob Erdmann, and editor, Glenn Austin, M.D., who believed in my idea and gave me the freedom to help make it a reality.

Acknowledgements

INTRODUCTION

Helping children develop positive TV habits is a challenge confronting every parent. Child experts tell parents to limit and monitor their children's TV viewing. If children were abusing a toy, the experts would suggest it be "put away." But TV is not a toy and it sits in the center of most homes tempting children to turn it on. *TV — Becoming Unglued* is a television planning system (TVPS) that shows parents not only how they can limit and monitor TV — it tells them how technology can help "put away" the TV and encourage family decision making.

TVPS (television planning system) is for "real" parents — parents like me, who love their kids, but don't always follow through with what they say, or wish they hadn't said what they did or, worst of all, don't remember what they said. They have "real" kids — kids who like doing what they want to do when they want to do it.

The creator of TVPS (TV Planning System) recognizes that each family is unique with its own set of values. TVPS is a structure for limiting TV time and a guide to developing critical viewing. It is not a prescription for what to select. TVPS is designed so that families can choose what they think is the best of TV.

Using TVPS helps families learn to make decisions and to critically question the programs they do watch. With TVPS, TV can become a privilege that enriches a child's life.

CONTENTS

THE TV DILEMMA

More homes have TV sets than indoor plumbing. In most homes, arguments about TV outnumber arguments about who's next in the bathroom. The TV dilemma echoes in the following comments of parents and children.

• Parents

Carol: "I don't know what I would do without the TV," says Carol, the mother of two children under 5. "My kids are into everything. If it's closed they open it. If it's full they empty it. I spend my days trying to avoid disaster. The only time I have a moment to myself is when the kids watch the tube. It helps me to cope!"

Sarah: Sarah, mother of three boys ages 12, 9, and 6, shakes her head, "I remember when I thought that way. Today, I hate what TV is doing to my family and me. I've become a video vigilante. My boys come home from school, grab a snack, scramble to the family room and turn on the set. If it's not cartoons, its Nintendo. Thirty minutes or an hour of relaxing is fine, but these kids would remain gazing open-mouthed at the TV until bedtime if I let them."

"When I tell the boys to go outside, out they go — for 15 minutes. If I get busy, these three noisemakers can silently re-enter the house, turn the set on, low, and be entrenched before I find them. 'Turn off the set' will be answered by 'But Mom, just let us see the end of this show,' or 'Just let me finish this game.' This dialog can rerun two to four times in an afternoon. By the time I get dinner ready, the fish isn't the only thing that feels fried."

"After dinner would be more of the same if I let them. Kids need to be outside playing with friends and getting some exercise. And when are they going to have time for homework and reading?"

Dave: "I wish I had your choice," responds Dave, the dad of Kathy, a thirteen-year-old. "I get home from work at 5:45 P.M. I want my daughter to do her homework and chores after school. Instead, she watches TV all afternoon. I've tried bribes and punishment — they don't work. In the evening when it would be nice to enjoy one another, I have to hound her about her homework. All she wants to do is watch more TV."

"Plus I'm concerned about what she watches. I talk with her about the shows it would be best to watch, but she is 13, she is curious, and I'm not there. I long for the days when my only concerns were Sesame Street and Mister Rogers!"

• Kids

Carrie: Carrie is 14 years old and her mom works part time. "I like TV. When I get home from school, the first thing I do is turn on the set. It makes it feel like someone's in the house. Besides, if it wasn't for TV, I'd be bored. Watching TV gives me something to do. After school, if Mom's not home, I like being able to decide what I'll watch.

I like zapping from station to station. You see some amazing things doing that."

Johnny: Johnny is 12 years old and sometimes his mom does volunteer work. "I really like video games 'cause I get to be part of the action. I'd play them all the time if Mom would let me."

"When she's busy she tells us to go watch TV. Then she'll read an article or hear a news show that says watching too much TV isn't good for kids. She'll be on our case for weeks. But she isn't home some days. Plus, if I keep turning on the set, she eventually gets tired and I get to watch."

These comments show some of the struggles families have as they try to live in harmony with the TV. Most parents enjoy seeing their children occupied and happy. Nintendo's popularity mushroomed because of these desires and because many parents could hardly wait to try the games themselves.

Parents' viewing habits can be role models for their children. Children have difficulty knowing how to behave when they receive conflicting messages. If parents watch TV every minute they are home, how can the child be expected to turn off the set when he has work to do? It also can be confusing when one minute Mom or Dad tells the kids to go watch TV and at another time they're instructed to stay away from the set. "Why?" is their logical question.

Watching TV can become a habit for many children — a habit many of them don't want to change. But kids who limit themselves to the 19-to-32 inch world of TV miss out on real life hands-on experiences.

TV is a window on the world. It exposes today's children to people, places and concepts known only by a few individuals in past generations. But looking through a window at children playing touch football is not the same as being part of the game. Watching people care about others on TV is not the same as caring for others or having people care for you. Even if all TV programs were outstanding, children's time in front of the set should be limited. Growing children need time to experience life. That's why child experts keep telling parents to limit and monitor their children's TV viewing.

When concerned parents do turn off the set, they're seldom met with, "Gee thanks, Mom, I needed that." Instead, parents confront statements like, "How can you be so mean?" "You're not fair," and "My friend Chuck gets to watch anytime he wants, why can't I?"

The easy choice is to let the kids watch whenever and whatever they want. Unfortunately, it's not best for the children. Saying "no" to excessive TV viewing is easier if parents understand what TV does to kids.

How to limit TV and at the same time use TV to teach children decision making and critical thinking skills is the main purpose of this book. It also shows how technology can conveniently "put away" the TV. *TV — Becoming Unglued* begins by examining what happens to children's bodies, minds and relationships when they sit glued to the tube for endless hours.

TIME FLIES—AND IT'S GONE

Time flies when kids watch TV. A common scenario: Child asks to play Nintendo for half an hour. Parent agrees. Parent becomes occupied. Two hours later "Super Mario" is still bouncing away. Children learn to tell time in first grade, but even teenagers can lose that ability in front of the TV set.

Since TV gained national pastime status, there have always been a few grandmothers, teachers, and even a few moms and dads that would say, "Johnny needs to be outside playing." Common sense told them kids needed to do something other than sit and gaze. Confronted with increasingly sophisticated video games and the cable smorgasbord, their common sense didn't always carry much authority.

Now child experts are vehemently saying the same thing. We listen to child experts because they study children's health and behavior. They measure, chart, and interpret intangibles like growth, fitness, and intelligence. These experts document what they say with their data, not just "common sense."

The American Academy of Pediatrics (AAP), 43,000 pediatricians concerned about the well-being of kids from infants to young adults, have studied children and television. In 1989 they found, "The average child in the United States still spent more time watching television than any other activity except sleeping."[1] According to the AAP, the typical youngster watches 3 to 3 1/2 hours of TV a day.

The 3 1/2 hours a day adds up to 7 full years in a 70-year life span.[2] In terms of real kids, the average means that for every child who watched 1 or 2 hours of TV a day, there is another child who spent 5 or 6 hours in front of the set. That figure does not include the time kids spend playing video games and watching videos.

So what? It's what happens to the bodies and minds of children as a result of sitting in front of the TV that concerns the experts. Three-and-a-half hour average may not sound so bad when parents think of Saturday or Sunday. But if they consider a school day, and add time in

school to time for eating and time for getting ready for bed, 3 1/2 hours becomes a large part of a day's free time. If the children go to bed at a reasonable hour, they don't have much time to do homework, read, or relate to the family. Also, when children sit in front of the tube, they often stuff their faces with fat-filled snacks.

In recent years as more adults tried to get in shape by walking and running, kids spent more time in front of the tube and got fatter. Doctors find that "television viewing . . . contributes substantially to obesity."[3] Obesity increased among children by 50 percent in the last two decades. According to Dr. William Dietz, director of clinical nutrition at the New England Medical Center in Boston, "Prevalence of obesity in 12 to 17 year olds increases by 2 percent for each hour of TV viewed daily."[4] However, excess weight is not the only problem.

Doctors predicted children with high cholesterol in 9 out of 10 cases by knowing the child's and family's medical history plus the child's TV habits.[5] Dr. Kurt Gold, the study coordinator at the University of California, Irvine, recommends pediatricians "ask about a child's TV viewing habits as a regular part of a physical exam to assess risk of premature heart disease."[6]

Obesity and heart disease are serious health problems at any age, but particularly for children. TV competes with playing and physical activity for kids' time. TV is winning and our kids are losing their fitness. The consequences of little physical activity are showing up in other places besides the doctor's offices.

The U.S. Army modified its basic training because so many recruits were being injured. "It's our opinion that the young people coming into the military now have spent more time in front of the TV than on the tennis court or a softball field," said Lt. Col. John Anderson, an Army podiatrist. In his 20-year career, he does not remember a time when recruits were in worse physical condition than they are now.[7]

Judy Griesheim, the chairman of physical education at Chicago's suburban Downers Grove South High School also has noticed a decrease in the strength and fitness of her students in the last few years.

"At 15 and 16 [years old] they should be at their prime, but sometimes I think that 30- and 40-year-olds can outrun them."[8] Today's 30- and 40-year olds may find this encouraging, but what will today's 16-year olds be like when they are 40?

A True Story from the Chicago Tribune

Rosann Barranco turned "sweet sixteen," happy because she was 50 not-so-sweet pounds lighter. A year ago Rosann would come home from school, watch TV and eat. "Those TV commercials can get you hungry," she says. "You'd see a cake and you'd want to go downstairs and get some." Today she has "nearly given up television, walks two miles every day, takes an aerobic dance class in school and has totally changed her approach to food."

Changing shape has given Rosann a new social life and focus. "She's a different child," says her mother, Ann. "She's happier. She's really come out of her shell." Rosann now thinks she would like to be a model and a nutritionist.[9]

Children's bodies numbed by video bombardment are not the only issue. Today's children are growing up in the midst of an information explosion. Is video mania preparing the majority of kids to enter a world where they will have to process and interpret more information than any generation before them? Education experts are doubtful.

SATs (Scholastic Aptitude Tests) are given each year to junior and senior high school students who wish to continue their education in college. These kids are usually among the brightest in school. Besides causing sweaty palms and nervous stomachs, these tests show how well students read and understand math principles. Since the test has been given for many years it also indicates how today's students compare with those that went to school years ago.

In 1990, the verbal SAT scores sank to a 10-year low. College Board president Donald M. Stewart, noted that reading could become a "lost art." He said students "must pay less attention to video games and music videos and begin to read more." The College Board report noted that "more than half of high school seniors read 10 or fewer pages a day and that one-third are not required to write even two paragraphs a week. But they average watching television at least three hours a day."[10]

> *"The man who does not read good books has no advantage over the man who can't read them."*
>
> Mark Twain

* Names used in true stories have been changed to protect the privacy of the families except for those quoted from the newspapers.

A True Story

What's a family to do when their daughter is in the lowest reading group in the primary grades? The answer for the Garetts came when business sent the family to live in Italy for two years. Since

WHY JOHNNY CAN'T READ AND WRITE

their daughter Lisa did not speak Italian, she thought Italian TV was boring. With TV eliminated as a time filler, Lisa discovered books and read during much of her free time. When Lisa returned to her old school in the states, her reading tests placed her in the top reading group.

Reading is a skill. To develop it requires effort, just as any other skill does. If you want to be a good basketball player, you practice basketball. If you want to be a good reader, you practice reading.

TV doesn't just affect children physically and mentally. It impacts them emotionally where they live in relationships to peers and family. Linda Ellerbee, TV commentator and author, shares her feelings about TV as a child in her book *Move On.* She says, "The August I was eight years old, a television ate my best friend."[11] Lucy was her "very first very best friend." They played cowboys, dodgeball, and spent hours talking while they swung on her "picture-perfect swing." Then Lucy's dad brought home a television.

*Maybe the TV hadn't actually eaten her. But she may as well
have been dead; once they pointed her in the direction of that
box, she never looked up and she never looked back. Every
afternoon when she got home from school, she'd sit down on
the floor in their living room and watch whatever there was to
watch. Every Saturday morning, she'd watch cartoons. I'm
not kidding when I say I lost my best friend.*[12]

Ellerbee tells of her loss, but imagine what her friend Lucy lost —
the chance to think, grow and experience real life with Linda. Ellerbee
also describes what TV did to her own family:

*Television changed my family forever. We stopped eating
dinner at the dining-room table after my mother found out
about TV trays....Dinner was served in time for one program
and finished in time for another. During dinner we used to
talk to one another. Now television talked to us. If you had
something you absolutely had to say, you waited until the*

*commercial, which is, I suspect, where I learned to speak in
thirty-second bursts. As a future writer, it was good practice
in editing my thoughts. As a little girl, it was as lonely as hell.
Once in a while, I'd pass our dining-room table and stop,
thinking I heard our ghosts sitting around talking to one
another, saying stuff....*

*Television was taking my parents away from me, not all
the time but enough, I believed. When it was on they didn't
see me, I thought.* [13]

The pain pictured in these comments happened approximately 30
years ago, yet it is so vivid. Imagine how it felt at the time. Ellerbee
compares life before and after TV. Many kids of today are weaned on
TV. They don't know what they are missing, but that doesn't mean the
family discussions and life experiences with best friends and are not
missed.

Watching TV can be an addictive passive experience — it requires no effort. Unfortunately, after people blob out in front of the TV, they have more difficulty concentrating and feel less alert. "The longer people look at television, the greater is the probability that they will continue to look."[14] Many parents came to that conclusion years ago.

No one can renew, reuse, or rerun time. Once it has passed it is gone forever. "If one of the goals of life is to realize one's latent potentialities, . . . then the *prolonged* and *indiscriminate* viewing of television is likely to present an obstacle in achieving that purpose."[15] (Emphasis added.) Watching TV may give kids some idea about what they would like to be, but it doesn't help them develop any skills, abilities or relationships that can lead them to their goal.

Children tend to focus on the here and now. They have difficulty understanding that choices have consequences, particularly if the consequences are not immediate. This is normal. Many would rather watch TV than do their homework. In their minds, what they do today is unrelated to their opportunities for tomorrow. Children accustomed to unlimited access to TV see little reason to stop or limit their viewing.

To sum up the problem — "Time spent watching television is time a child isn't outdoors playing or inside with a book. All this television watching is stealing away from children the time they need to spend just being children, having the experiences of being a kid." These are the words of Dr. Robert A. Mendelson, the pediatrician who chaired the American Academy of Pediatrics committee on communications in 1990.[16]

Most child experts are not opposed to television. What concerns them is *excessive* unmonitored TV use. Unfortunately, because children lack "experience, education, and self-control, [they] are among the most likely of groups to become indiscriminate heavy viewers of television."[17] They need the help and guidance of their parents and caring adults.

As we prepare to enter the 21st century, television technology is making TV viewing increasingly captivating. High definition television (HDTV) will make the pictures on very large screens exceptionally clear. According to William Connolly, president of Sony Advanced Systems Company and former head of research for CBS, the structure of the viewing angle will draw the viewer more into the picture.[18] What does this mean for families? It probably means limiting children's TV viewing is not going to get easier, which increases the concern of parents and experts about what TV teaches kids. This topic is the subject of the next chapter.

TV THE EDUCATOR: WHO'S CHOOSING THE CURRICULUM?

TV is a master story teller. Its stories come complete with moving color pictures that captivate and influence the way all of us think. "Television is, for better or worse, a prime educator."[19]

When parents think of TV, the educator, they think of Sesame Street. Big Bird, Oscar the Grouch, and Cookie Monster, along with gyrating letters, teach kids the alphabet as well as shapes, colors, and much more. Sesame Street is a kaleidoscope of fun that educates.

Parents also think of Mr. Rogers talking to children about friendship, or National Geographic Specials showing whales roaming the oceans or spiders burying themselves in desert sands. These are positive examples of TV's potential. But TV teaches other lessons almost every second the current lights the screen.

Its effectiveness is measured in the competitive system of our economy. Each year cereal and toy manufacturers pay TV networks millions to run ads that educate kids and adults about their products. If they did not make a profit on their investment of TV advertising dollars, we wouldn't see products by the same manufacturers year after year on the tube.

The Streets and Sanitation workers in Melbourne, Australia, can also document the power of the media to educate: "They now must put up with teenagers Down Under [literally!]. Some youths are taking to the city's sewers on bicycles and skateboards as their contribution to the Teen-age Mutant Ninja Turtles craze."[20] Kids, bikes, skateboards, and sewers have existed for decades. It took the media to bring them together. We may chuckle at this example, but the sanitation workers worry that someone will be seriously injured or killed by a flash flood or by sewer gas.

Back in the States, U.S. libraries reported a 500 percent increase in library card applications following an episode of "Happy Days." Fonzie, the main character, took out a library card — the viewers followed his example.[21]

TV influences all of us: "Psychologists, educational experts, and TV critics say the shows you and your family watch can affect your opinions, your relationships — even your behavior and that of your kids."[22] So, what is TV teaching and not teaching us and our children?

Many parents and child experts don't like what TV is offering in the name of entertainment. Mike Royko, a hard-nosed newspaper columnist, described flipping through some major cable channels:

> *"Flip. There's somebody being shot or blown up.*
> *Flip. There are a couple of people stripping and hopping in bed.*
> *Flip. There are a couple of people in bed being shot or blown up.*
> *Flip. Ah. what a relief. It's a standup comedian. But what's that he's saying? The old "F" word? Not once, not twice. Goodness, doesn't he know any other words? Of course he does. Now he's using the "MF" word."*[23]

Blood, guts, and sex are major themes of many TV shows. By the time kids graduate from high school they will have witnessed 18,000 murders. Each year "American teenagers see an estimated 14,000 sexual references and innuendoes."[24]

The Annenburg School of Communications in Philadelphia found that "55 percent of prime-time characters are involved in violent confrontations once a week." If they were depicting the real world it would happen less than one per cent of the time.[25] Why should this concern parents?

As far back as 1972, the Surgeon General reported that data left no doubt "there is a definite link between violence on TV and violence in some children."[26] The American Academy of Pediatrics in 1990 said, "Sufficient data have accumulated to warrant the conclusion that protracted television viewing is one cause of violent or aggressive behavior."[27]

The relationship between watching violence and aggressive behavior is very complicated. However, the studies seem to indicate violent behavior in some children is encouraged by what they view on the TV screen. Other experts suggest that children who repeatedly view violent scenes can become overly fearful or, conversely, insensitive.[28]

Some studies show children in kindergarten frequently can't tell if violence on TV results from characters trying to help or harm other people. What the children seem to remember is the excitement associated with the aggression. Children can also think that verbal assults — the put-downs or caustic comments, sometimes overlayed with laugh tracks, are funny phrases many people use to relate to each other. They don't understand that in the real world relationships can be destroyed with these types of comments.

And what about sex and drugs? In 1986 the pediatricians felt that TV presented sex and drug use in "realistic or inviting terms." Because this was happening so frequently, they thought kids might get the message that "everybody does it." They noted, "Television characters rarely say 'no.'"[29] With the high incidence of teen-age pregnancy and

deaths from drunk driving, the doctors think we should be concerned. These messages do not help lessen the spread of AIDS either.

The *USA TODAY* cover story on November 2, 1988 was "Tabloid TV: 'Now you see it on the air.'" One of the cover stories on January 7, 1989, *TV GUIDE* was "TV's Getting Sexier . . . How Far Will It Go?" Both articles state how "former taboos have become acceptable." The networks are pushing to see how much nudity, kinky sex, and profanity the audience will accept during prime time. In their quest for ratings, they omit the basic positive values.

Television critic Jeff Greenfield, notes how many producers seem to have forgotten the basic issues:

> *"They have moved into areas once considered untouchable in prime time; yet the most common, most crucial area of all time — the capacity of modern men and women to love, trust, share, and provide a moral framework for children, this seems to be beyond their grasp."* [30]

What children see on TV is important because they are so vulnerable. Young children view TV as a window on reality. For them, watching TV is like looking in a neighbor's window with the volume turned up. One day a young child asked Mr. Rogers, "How did you get out of the TV?"[31] The child didn't realize he was looking at a picture. He thought Mr. Rogers actually lived inside the set.

Young children tend to believe that what they are viewing is true, whether it is a commercial, cartoon, or murder mystery. They can become frightened by the the content because they are confused by what's shown. Children under age 7 have limited real life experiences to compare with what they see on TV. Therefore, they assume what they see on the tube is real: "One-third of seven-year-olds think characters like Doogie Howser, M.D., are real."[32] "A witch on the screen is just as alive and terrifying to a child as a flesh-and-blood burglar would be to you."[33]

A True Story

*Seven year old Emily from the East Coast went to visit her
Aunt Ellen and Uncle Rick in the southwest. They decided to
treat her to a trip to the north rim of the Grand Canyon.
Driving from Flagstaff, Arizona, to the canyon Uncle Rick
commented they were in the Painted Desert. Emily protested,
"This isn't a desert. It doesn't look like the desert I've seen on
TV." Uncle Rick explained that not all deserts looked alike,
but he could not convince her. Emily insisted he was wrong,
that she had never been to the desert. The desert she had seen
on TV was more real to her than reality itself.*

Some older children also believe the world they see on TV is more
real than the world they can touch and smell. "Sometimes the fiction
of television becomes the standard by which actual experiences are
gauged."[34] Unfortunately, the influence of TV continues to grow

"with the decline of the extended family and its support systems . . . as people look to the tube for role models."[35]

Herbert London, dean of New York University's Gallatin Division, interviewed 24 representative high school students from Brooklyn to discover the influence of TV on their social attitudes. His conclusion was that "...television is having a profound effect on the values of young Americans," regardless of their economic, racial or ethnic backgound.[36]

The popular "heroes" of today's students often have their immoral behavior "sumptuously rewarded." Kids are viewing these characters as role models. One young woman described Alexis of "Dynasty" as bad, evil, vicious, bold, glamorous and calculating; then said, "...she's everything any woman would want to be." A young man commented that he "sort of" admired J.R. Ewing of "Dallas," "...the way he can corrupt everybody and not even let it affect him." Most of the students thought these programs show how business people really behave. All the students agreed they would act immorally if that was the only way to keep a business going even though their parents would disapprove of such actions.[37]

Kids watch shows and commercials attentively. They want to see what adults think is important, how men, women, and children relate, and how minorities interact. Kids learn what clothing and hair styles are "in," how language, sarcasm, and now profanity are used, and what types of people our society values.

Young people seen on the TV screen may represent to kids the way children "should" behave. Mental health professionals believe the more children and adults identify with the families and people seen on TV, the greater the impact on their behavior.

Concerned parents need to make deliberate choices about what their families watch. What is on TV is not controlled by them or their children. Therefore parents in a sense, choose a curriculum by the programs they allow to be viewed in their home — a curriculum that has a very powerful means of delivery.

In making choices they will want to consider the age of the children and the values and behaviors that are important to their family. Values omitted as well as values presented are worth noting. As Fred Rogers stated in his book, *Mister Rogers Talks To Parents*, too often TV "doesn't give much chance to talk about love, compassion, commitment, integrity, the preciousness of life — all the many things that help make us feel good about being individual, unique human beings."[38]

THE TELEVISION PLANNING SYSTEM (TVPS)
Becoming Unglued

Once kids are glued to the tube, ungluing them requires some effort. Kids like TV and see no reason to turn it off. The goal is to help the child enjoy and learn from the best of TV, yet have time to grow by experiencing the joys and pains of living in the real world.

It's helpful for parents to remember that "...unrestricted exposure to television does not teach children to be more discriminating viewers. Nor does it help them acquire general knowledge or a better grasp of plots, commercials or special effects."[39]

Help children understand TVPS (The Television Planning System), is for their benefit. It's not a punishment! It's not a parental power play! Parents can be sensitive to their children's feelings. They can share some of the information presented in the previous chapters. If the children are in early grade school, parents can read them *The Wretched Stone* by Chris Van Allsburg (Houghton Mifflin Company, 1991). The story is based on a ship captian's log and tells of a talented crew finding a luminous rock two feet across and bringing it on the ship. What happens to the crew as they become captivated with the rock can naturally lead to a family discussion about limiting TV viewing.

The TV Planning System (TVPS) is designed to minimize battles and to be fair. Respect for the child and his or her opinions is central to this plan. Kids are more apt to cooperate if they help develop the plan. Psychologists would say give the kids ownership of some of the decisions.

Families with several children may have one child who wants to spend most of his/her time in front of the set. It's best not to call attention to this child but to treat the TVPS approach as a family effort. Try to involve the entire family and be sensitive to each person's wishes.

• The Way We Are

Before you begin TVPS (TV Planning System), record the amount of time your family spends in front of the set (TV, Nintendo, and tapes). Parents tend to underestimate how much TV their children watch. Some studies indicate they err by as much as 50%.

On the following page marked "THE WAY WE ARE," record the amount of time your family spends in front of the TV for one week. As your family begins TVPS, they will be able to refer back to this sheet to measure their improvement.

THE WAY WE ARE

Before you start the Television Planning System (TVPS), record the amount of time your family spends in front of the set (TV, Nintendo, and tapes) for a seven day period. Later you will be able to refer to this page to measure the progress your family makes.

Week of _____ to _____

Sunday's total _____ hrs. _____ min.

Monday's total _____ hrs. _____ min.

Tuesday's total _____ hrs. _____ min.

Wednesday's total_____ hrs. _____ min.

Thursday's total _____ hrs. _____ min.

Friday's total _____ hrs. _____ min.

Saturday's total _____ hrs. _____ min.

Actual Total Tube Time _____Hours _____Min.

• Limiting TV Time

The Basic Plan

(Forms to be used with this section are found in appendix II.)

At the beginning of each week, the family decides how much Total TUBE TIME (shows, video tapes, and games) to be scheduled. Enter this amount on the week's record under "GOAL FOR WEEK'S TOTAL TUBE TIME." Each family's needs and expectations are different. There is no right answer to the amount of time, however most child experts recommend no more than 2 hours a day for children and that TV not be watched during meals.

On the daily TVPS record, (Appendix II) write the name of the program, game, or tape and figure the number of hours and minutes for each selection. Total the time watched each day and enter that amount on the weekly record. At the end of the week total the ACTUAL TOTAL TUBE TIME. The family may wish to evaluate how successful they have been in meeting their goal.

Poker chips can be used as a visual aid to help younger children understand time limits. At the beginning the week, each child is given chips representing the total amount of time they may watch TV that week (each red chips represents 60 minutes and each white chip 30 minutes). A jar with a slit in the top is placed on the TV. When the child goes to watch, he deposits the appropriate chips. When all the chips are gone, there is no more TV for that week.

or

The TV Diet

If that's too drastic for your family, use TVPS to go on a "TV diet." Use the TVPS record (Appendix II) to write down the program, tape and game times your family watch. Then systematically cut back one event a week (or month) until you reach what you think is a desirable amount of ACTUAL TOTAL TUBE TIME.[40]

or

Earn Tube Time

Have your children earn their TV time — allow TV to be a reward. Rewards are not given to force good behavior. Instead, rewards are given because the children accepted responsibility and met an agreed upon objective standard. For instance one agreement could be if the children read for 30 minutes, they get to watch an hour of TV. If the children don't read or do agreed upon chores, they get no TV. It doesn't matter if mom's had a bad day. The children are given the power to choose. "An appropriate reward used as honest pay induces positive future behavior in children."[41]

To avoid misunderstandings, write down the terms of the agreement and have both parents and children sign it. This approach can be used with homework and chores as well. This process also lets children

know that parents place a higher priority on school work and other creative and physical activities than they do on watching TV.

Enter the programs the children plan to earn on the TVPS Daily Record (Appendix II). As they complete the task and enjoy the program, tape or game, record Total Time where indicated. At the end of the week, enter the daily times of the weekly record and compute the ACTUAL TOTAL TUBE TIME. Use the TVPS Record to affirm their hard work.

> *"The most valuable lesson you can teach your child is that privileges and freedoms are tied to responsible behavior."*[42]

It is NOT recommended that watching TV be used as a bribe: "A bribe is given to a child while she's behaving badly, in the hope that she'll stop."[43] If little Sally is crying for candy, don't say, "If you stop crying, I'll let you watch TV."

Under the pressure of confrontation, it's tempting for parents to use not watching TV as a punishment. DON'T! If Johnny breaks a lamp bouncing a basketball in the living room, don't tell him he can't watch TV because he didn't listen. "The major problem with the popular view of punishment is that it is associated with anger and retaliation. In effect punishment is viewed as a way the parents 'get back' at the child for some bit of misbehavior."[44] If parents discipline this way, they will have greater difficulty getting their children to cooperate with TVPS. Instead, decide on a consequence that relates to the misbehavior.

• Decisions, Decisions — What to Watch

Learning to make decisions is designed into many school curricula. If children can watch TV only for a limited time, they learn to decide which shows they really want to see. The process of deciding and planning teaches them valuable lessons.

At the beginning of the week, the family selects programs from a TV listing guide and writes them as well as the games and tapes in the TVPS Daily Record (Appendix II). Note when the program begins and ends so the TUBE TIME can be determined. If disagreements develop during the week, have each member of the family sign the record the next week. This step indicates everyone understands the agreement.

Many program selections will be determined by the age of the children. The parent's role is like that of an interior decorator helping a client decorate his home — limiting his selections so he can pick the best of the best.

Let older children make choices from acceptable alternatives. Keep in mind that in the playgrounds, halls and cafeterias of our schools TV shows are one of the main topics of conversation. Try to understand your child's point of view. This does not mean you change your values, only that you discuss your differences. (Please consult the next chapter, Becoming Media Smart for more pointers in this area.)

A VCR can help families have more flexibility in planning and watching TV. Quality shows that are aired at inconvenient times can be recorded and viewed when the family desires. Video stores and libraries contain countless program selections and games that can be incorporated into the viewing plan.

Turn the TV on only for agreed upon programs, etc. It may be helpful to use a timer to signal the end of an agreed upon program time. This helps to de-personalize the situation.   The goal is for families to watch specific programs not just watch TV.

Be cautiously flexible. There may be some special programs (championship sporting events or a special mini series) that park your family in front of the tube longer than you like. One way to handle this is to adjust time allowed for other programs and video games. These exceptions should be permitted judiciously or they can become all too common.

• Putting the TV Away

The children and parents in the Johnson family agree to limit their TV time and the programs for the week are selected. Wednesday, the TV is to go on at 7:00 P.M.

Wednesday afternoon at 3:35 P.M. eleven-year-old Brad Johnson enters an empty house. His mom has taken Susie, his sister, to her music lesson and won't be back until 5:30 P.M. The house seems particularly quiet. Thank goodness for Fritz, the family dog.

Brad drops his book bag, marches to the kitchen, opens the frige, grabs a gallon of milk, and pours some into a glass. Off comes the head of the lion cookie jar, and in plunges Brad's hand to retrieve a fist full of his favorite cookies. As he begins to munch away, Brad's eye catches sight of the blank TV screen in the adjoining family room.

Brad remembers the cartoons he likes watching in the afternoon. Sure, he had agreed to eliminate them when everyone decided no more than two hours of TV a day. The Wednesday night shows are the ones he really wants to see. But no one is home — who would know? Yes, he has school work due tomorrow, he is supposed to practice the trumpet and put away his folded wash, but it is so quiet. Brad walks into the family room and turns on the set.

Other children, either because of temperment or because of past history with the parents, view attempts to modify their behavior as a test. The parenthood job description for many parents includes being tested by their kids. Stories of parental testing are frequently heard in groups of commiserating parents. Mixed feelings are common — "I can't believe my kid would do such a thing" — "That little stinker is really creative." Testing stories color much adult conversation and stir parental memories of how they tested their own parents.

Some kids like being in control. TV sitcoms reinforce this idea. The following true story may give some TV writers an idea.

A True Story from Louisville, Kentucky

Pam and Joe Severson argued with their children about TV for the last time. Joe unplugged the set and hauled it to the garage.

*He thought that if it stayed there for a while maybe his kids
would believe Pam when she said, "No TV!"*

*Two weeks later, Pam went to the garage to search for
the trowel she needed to plant flowers. As she opened the
garage door, her mouth dropped open. There sat her startled
children in front of the tube. They had connected the set with
the outdoor extension cord.*

Experts say limit TV viewing, but no one suggests how to limit access
to the TV. If children were over-indulging on candy or abusing a toy,
the experts would suggest that the parents put it away. Parents would
be encouraged to discuss appropriate behavior and consequences with
their children. At a later time, the candy or toy would be re-introduced
with a reminder about what is expected. This method would be
repeated until the child adopted appropriate behavior.

But where do you put away a TV? And, who is going to carry it
there? So, there in the middle of the home sits the TV, just waiting to

be turned on. If mom and dad work, or are out, or busy, it sure is tempting to see what's on.

How do you limit access to the TV? Families with young children may find covering the set with a spread or throw is enough of a deterrent. There are a few cabinets and entertainment centers that are secured with a key.

Technology is beginning to respond to the plight of hassled families. Families can now free their children's minds from wondering what will appear on the screen when the TV "on" button is pulled. Three products are available that lock onto the power cord of the TV and determine if the TV receives electricity. If families have VCRs, all three products allow them to record programs even when the TV cannot be turned on.

The Switch ($25.00 post-paid) is a basic electrical device that regulates the flow of electricity to the TV with a key. When the key is turned to "off", the TV cannot be turned on because it is not receiving electrical power. The TV operates regularly when the key is in the "on" position.

If Brad's family had used The Switch, Brad would have marched into the family room, pulled the "on" button and nothing would have happened. He probably would have finished his cookies and maybe done his homework.

SuperVision (around $100.00) is a programmable accesory that also operates via the electrical cord of the TV. This unit can turn the electricity to the TV on and off for two different time periods during each day. Families can assign a specific time allowance to each child (up to 4 children) that can vary from day to day. The unit allows the child to watch for only the assigned amount of "on" TV time. However, children can be given a wide or narrow range of choices within those limits. Much of the record keeping of TVPS (Television Planning System) can be programmed into this device. Daily and weekly time totals are automatically monitored and tabulated. Parents are told how they can override the system at any time. A visual display activated by a password leads parents through the programming process.

TimeSlot (around $100.00) also is a programmable device that allows the TV to be turned on and off at specific times. It too keeps track of the amount of time each child watches the set. Instead of a password, TimeSlot uses a coded card, much like building security passcard systems, to activate the program. Eight different coded cards are available so eight children can be given time alotments. Each time the child activates the TV with his card, the unit deducts the time from his daily or weekly allowance. Parents program this unit by inserting an administrator card and then following the display's instructions.

If Brad's family had SuperVision or TimeSlot attached to their TV, Brad could have watched his favorite afterschool cartoon for half an hour. The TV would be programed to turn off when the cartoon was over, and Brad hopefully would decide to do his homework. The thirty

*The Television
Planning System*

minutes he did watch would have been deducted from his daily allotment.

To the author's knowledge, these are the only three products designed to aid families in developing positive viewing habits (See Appendix I). There is a product called Homework First ($19.95), but it only limits the use of Nintendo. Technology can help families! Hopefully, other new products will appear to help families plan their viewing. Ideally, a special VCR could be designed where families could program and lock in both channel and time.

Does this approach work? Thousands of parents who wanted to free their children from the TV habit and encourage them to become selective viewers have purchased The Switch. Comments from a couple of these parents show how reasonable limitation of TV is received by some children.

True Stories

From Vineland, New Jersey
"TV Lockout" by Sandy Bauers
Philadelphia Inquirer, May 8, 1990, p. 1-D
Reprinted with permission fromThe Philadelphia Inquirer.

*Frank Giovanelli was so stunned, he barely argued with her.
It wouldn't have changed anything anyway. His mother was
too determined. Twelve-year-old Frank had been spending
most of every evening planted in front of the TV, "mesmerized
....He wouldn't even listen to you when you talked to him,"
said Rebecca Schumann, of Vineland. On school holidays,
when her son was home alone, she'd drop by during her lunch
break and find him watching "Divorce Court."*

*Schumann bought The Switch, a device that blocked the
power to the TV with a simple turn of the key....*

*"During that month last fall, we talked about a lot of
different things," she said. "I gave him a lot of things to
read."*

*Today, Frank sets his own TV schedule — "he can watch
as long as his chores and his homework are done" —
Schumann says he's "using more intelligence" in making his
selections. Still she closely monitors her son's viewing, and if
she thinks he's tuning in too much or to the wrong show, "we
talk about it."*

(Several weeks after the article appeared, Schumann said she was able to
leave The Switch "on" most of the time.)

From Detroit, Michigan
"TV Turnoff", by Karen Bellenir
The Detroit News and *Free Press*, March 4, 1990, p. 5L.

*Like many parents, Lora Allen felt that limiting television and
monitoring programs were good ideas. But as a single parent*

with an outside job, she just couldn't be home all the time.

'At one point, I simply put the TV up in the top of my bedroom closet,' she recalls. "It was there for well over a year."

That's when Allan, who lives in Westland, read about a product called The Switch....

She says the device 'allows us to be more selective in our viewing. The TV doesn't go on unless it's for a specific pro gram, or video or Nintendo game.'

Connie Crowl of Ferndale bought The Switch last fall:'it's something so simple and it does do much....'

She uses The Switch to make sure her children do their homework before the television goes on.

'It made a statement. It said "Hey, homework is important...."

TV — BECOMING UNGLUED began when the author, mother of three sons, became frustrated with attempts to limit and monitor TV in her own home. Her sons' TV habits got out of hand when the youngest had serious medical problems for two years. "Go watch TV," she told the older boys while she coped with stress.

After two years her youngest son was well, but his brothers' TV habits were not. Tired of arguing about TV, she pleaded with her husband to "Do Something!" He cut off the TV plug, wired the set to a switch activated by a key which he encased in an electrical outlet box — truly ugly, but it worked.

The boys saw the programs they wanted and the "I'm bored" — click — on goes the TV," was eliminated. Studying, activities and reading took its place.

While researching the possibility of designing a product to help families with TV, the author found The Switch. During the past three years, she has tried to let families know about the product. This book combines research plus feedback from thousands of phone calls and letters she's received about this product. Yes — this method does work!

• "I'm Bored" — Finding Alternative Activities

As the TV clicks off, the words, "I'm bored" are uttered before the tube is cool. These words need to be taken seriously according to writer Alan Caruba who has researched boredom. He says boredom "...is the background music to a lot of social problems." It has been linked to school drop out, violence by youth gangs, and depression. Caruba believes many people are bored because they are encouraged to be "spectators in the lives of others," instead of learning to enrich their own lives.[45] Sitting and gazing at the tube reinforces the spectator syndrome.

Encourage children to experiment with their creativity and imagination. Ask children the kinds of things they like to do. List alternative activities. Collect art and craft supplies and any other equipment like boxes and blankets so they can create a picture or their own world of villains and heroes. Store these items in a box. Younger children might enjoy having a box for them labeled (Child's name)'s Entertainment Center. The book, *365 TV-Free Activities You Can Do With Your Child*, by Steve and Ruth Bennett is a helpful resource. (It is published by Bob Adams, Inc. and can be ordered by calling 800-872-5627.)

Some families have found it helpful at first to set aside half an hour each day to show their children how to use some of their supplies and to try different types of play. After doing this for awhile, they have found their children get used to the idea of creative play.

Have children select books, magazines and newspapers from the library or store to keep on hand. *The New Read-Aloud Handbook* by Jim Trelease (Penquin Books, 1989) is an excellent reading resource book. Sometimes a TV show can introduce a subject children might want to read about. "It is reading, not watching TV, that will provide the real information and the entertainment (they) need to enrich (their lives.")[46]

Substitution is essential to an effective cutback in viewing. You can have a family discussion about "the best times of my life have been . . . ." What usually comes out of these discussions is that the things we enjoy and remember the most are those that "require concentrated skill, that do not separate the individual from the end result of his or her effort." These activities that require focused attention also provide the exhilarations that make life interesting.[47]

What happens when families cut back on their TV vewing? In *The No TV Week: Unplugging the Plug-In Drug*, author Marie Winn reports the results of a "No TV Week" sponsored by schools throughout the country. The purpose of the "week" was to help families discover what they were missing. The comments that follow are instructive:

"The week I turned off my television I read more books, my school grades got a little better, I practiced piano more, I also learned to knit, I played a lot of indoor games with my sister and brothers, I got to know my family and myself better."

Sixth grader, Richmond, Indiana[48]

"I didn't realize how much I used the TV to entertain the kids and keep them quiet. I was amazed at how creative the girls were when TV was not an option.

Mother, Marshall, Missouri[49]

"Now that I couldn't watch TV I thought of other things to do.... I read all the books that I had classified as 'boring' and discovered how good they really were."

Sixth grader, Marshall, Missouri[50]

Research reported in *Television and the Quality of Life* by Robert Kubey and Mihaly Csikszentmihalyi seems to agree with what these families say: "Parents who have suddenly removed the set, although reporting many initial difficulties in adjustment, also report increases in the amount of time devoted to reading and hobbies, as well as joint activities and family communication."[51]

While TVPS does not advocate getting rid of the set, families can enjoy many of the same benefits by limiting the amount of time they spend in front of the tube. The key is planning. Learning to use TV to benefit your family instead of mindlessly abdicating their minds to the whims of TV advertisers and producers, requires that we educate ourselves and our children to think critically about what we see on the set.

Becoming Media Smart:
Developing Critical Thinking Skills

Walter Cronkite's famous sign off, "And that's the way it is," describes how most of us looked at TV during its first 40 years. We didn't much question what we saw — we were entertained, captivated. The crude technology of early TV made it easier for our minds to separate reality from the world of TV. New technology blurs that separation, and it is critical we teach our children to question what they see. We need to teach them to be media smart.

The screens aren't just becoming larger and the pictures sharper (high definition TV — HDTV). Computers with "CD-ROMS" and "videodiscs" wired to TV monitors put text, graphics, sounds and video at users' fingertips (interactive TV). A lesson in Shakespeare could include structural drawings of famous Shakespearean theaters, displays of costumes, and soliloquies delivered by Lawrence Olivier in addition to the text. The only limitation is the creativity of the software developer.

Technicians are breaking through to "virtual reality." The participant views through a helmet and wears a data glove. He experiences the sensation of being an active part of an artificial three dimensional environment that mimicks real life. "In a program already produced by the University of Washington, a visitor 'flies' like Superman over Seattle skyscrapers, hearing the sound of chattering diners in the Space Needle restuarant as he zips by. If he points his forefinger downward he soon finds himself underwater in Puget Sound, where two playful, clicking whales swim alongside for company."[52] The game possibilities with this technology are "virtually" unlimited. Predictions are it will be on the market in two years. Some think it could become "...a new kind of electronic LSD."[53]

The glow of the TV screen no longer confines itself to the home, hospital room, and waiting room. Supermarket videos demonstrate how to prepare kiwi fruit while department store display monitors play style shows and instruct how to accessorize with scarves. The blank TV that sat in the back of the classroom is coming alive with programs developed for schools by CNN, Discovery Channel, Learning Channel and others. Eighty-five per cent of the nations' public schools have access to cable programming.[54]

The potential for media in the classroom is exciting, yet somewhat frightening. The possibilities for media manipulation increase, especially since young children believe so much of what they see on the screen. So what are we to do? TV is not going away nor would we want it to! We and our children need to be aware of how the media shapes our world. Becoming a critical TV viewer is the first step.

• Let's Talk

"The box that talks is also a box to talk about."[55] As parents interpret and explain to their young children what is on TV, they help to shape

their children's values. TV also can be a shared experience parents use to help their children develop decision- making and critical-thinking skills. Learning to question and discuss what's on TV can stimulate thinking that can transfer to school work as well.

After watching a short sitcom, weekly series or cartoon together the parents can try to help their children talk about the show by gently prompting them with the following questions. The age of the children will determine how complete and accurate the answers will be.

1. Who are the characters in the show?
   Ask the children to describe their appearance and actions.

2. Where did the episode take place?

3. What was the situation this week?

4. What happened?
   —Note the sequence of events
   —What was the most important part of the story?

5. Why do you think it happened?

As the children get older, you can add the next questions.

6. If you were the main character, would you have made that
   choice? Why? Why not?

7. Do you know anyone who would make a choice like that?

Take clues from the children's body language and partial phrases, then restate the children's answers to make sure you understood their point. Above all, respect your children enough to listen. Kids get lost in details — expect that. To young children the details are the show. Try to help them string the details together with a common thread. Do not be too anxious to correct them.

Make this a special time for the children. Use this format with the same show for several weeks so it's easier for the children to remember the characters. Check your local TV listings to see if there are comments about the show. Ask the children if they agree with those comments.

At a later time, ask the children to explain a show you didn't see with them. At first use the same series you used before so they have an easier time remembering the characters. This puts your children center stage and they become the teacher. Your role is to encourage them to expand and explain their concepts. Once children learn how to discuss one type of show, experiment using the same questions with different types of shows.

If you want a less structured discussion, try the following game.

Media Skill Builder: Rate That Show

Purpose: To provide cues for discussing the show later.

Give each viewer a stack of 3 by 5 cards or squares of colored paper. Write one word or phrase per card. As viewers watch the show, have each one select two or three words or phrases they think best describes the program. After the show is over, use the words as cues for lively family discussion.

funny	nice	unbelievable
too silly	too many put downs	powerful

too bloody	impossible	dramatic
scary	clever	stupid
exciting	sad	

Be sure you respect your children's opinions.

• The VCR—A Tool for Media Education

TV parents, like the Huxtables on the "Cosby Show," always respond with the perfect retort to the unexpected situation. Real families don't have scripts or the luxury of editing discussions that don't flow. However, parents can think through how they want to respond to controversial programs by first recording and then previewing the shows.

— Does the program provide important information?

— Have some facts been omitted?

— Does the program reflect the family's values?
   Why or why not?

— Would anyone respond in real life like the character
in the TV show?
— Would you want your child to respond like the characters
in the show?

If the family does decide to watch the show, they can stop the tape and discuss the areas of concern.

The VCR can also help with the now-you-see-it, now-you-don't speed of TV. Some programs present so much information so quickly that adults have difficulty processing it. For children, it is almost impossible. Before one concept is absorbed the next one is on the screen. By recording the program on the VCR, families can watch the program again, stopping the tape to discuss various points and examining special effects and media techniques. Commercials can also be critiqued or fast forwarded. (An excellent source on media techniques is *Use TV to Your Child's Advantage* by Dorothy and Jerome Singer, Acropolis Press, 1990.)

• Controversial News, Documentaries, and Dramas

Writers and reporters, the creators of dramas and documentaries, have opinions just like you and I, especially when they have in-depth knowledge of a subject. Some of them promote their opinions while entertaining us with their programs. Viewers frequently look at shows unaware of the biases written into the scripts.

Everything we see and hear on TV is edited. Decisions have been made about which facts to include, which facts not to mention or edit out, which camera angle to shoot from, which camera footage to include, and which to omit. Some of these decisions are forced because of the limited amount of time the producers have to cover the information. Whatever the reason, subjective choices have been made.

Visual statements about controversial issues also influence our opinions. The TV camera lens is small. It cannot capture every angle. What we see on TV is what the camera person has decided to frame. We need to notice picture angles and how the pictures are strung together. "The increasing manipulation of the live lens by politicians and ideologues worldwide makes it even more essential that we carefully sort through the melange of images, that we listen as well as watch, and that we turn the television off every so often to think about what we have seen."[56]

All of us, including our children, can evaluate programs dealing with social issues using the following questions:

1. What did the writers of this show think of the situation?
   — How are they defining their terms?

2. How do we know what the writers are saying is true?
   — What facts have they included?
   — Have they omitted any important facts?
   — Do we know of someone with first hand experience?
      Would they agree or disagree with the point of view?
   — Does the print media agree?

3. If what the writers say is true, what does it mean?
   —How would the writers like to resolve the issue?

4. What if the show is only partially true or not true at all?

5. Do the pictures appear to be taken in, or out of context?
   —Do the pictures match what the words are saying?
   —Have any obvious pictures been left out?

• Is It for Real?

Special effects make much of TV a land of make believe, or at least, a distortion of reality. Camera angles can make a handful of people look like a huge demonstration or a toy truck look like an 18 wheel semi. Laugh tracks sometimes convince us we missed something funny because we hear the "audience" laughing. Scary and romantic music

colors our emotions as we watch some ordinary events in a story. The sophisticated computer-generated effects like those seen in the movies "Star Wars" and "Terminator II" also play tricks with our minds.

TV is an art form that attempts to control the perceptions of the viewer. If children develop some awareness of special effects, they are less likely to be manipulated by them. Children in the upper grades might want to research, "How TV Makes Us Believe — Special Effects." The following game helps make children aware of this TV magic:

Media Skill Builder: Become A Technical Critic

Purpose: To help kids understand what's really happening.

TV programs differ in type, story line, characters, setting etc. However, there are several technical similarities between like shows, e.g., evening news, sitcoms, police shows. Have your family identify and count (if it occurs more than once) some of the following technical items. If you think of others, add them to the list.

shoot-outs

romantic music

laugh-tracks

close-ups

scary music

women in make-up

special lighting

impossible car stunts

news anchors looking at the camera

Example: Note what happens on the show each time the music changes. What are they trying to make us believe?

• Commercials

No area is more artfully contrived than commercials. "Television is the most successful marketing device ever invented."[56] TV stations pay for program production by selling commercial time. The station is actually selling the attention of a defined audience it has captured with its programs. For example, Saturday morning the stations sell the attention of our children to the cereal and toy manufacturers.

Advertising is expensive. One estimate is that advertisers pay between $200,000 and $1,000,000 per minute of air time depending on the size of the audience. [57] Advertising agencies are paid added thousands of dollars to design commercials to persuade us to buy a company's product. Companies spend big bucks because they make even bigger bucks after their commercials appear on TV.

Children are particularly vulnerable to commercial messages. Remember, children under 5 usually cannot tell the difference between the program and the commercial. Both seem real to them.

The following games are designed to make children more aware of how commercials are used.

Media Skill Builder: Place Those Ads

Purpose: To help kids note when commercials start and end. They become more aware that TV is a money-making operation and hopefully think to question motives.

Ten minutes before the show begins, give each viewer a piece of paper and a pencil. Ask viewers to pretend they work for an ad agency. Announce the name and/or type of show they are about to watch and have players guess the types of ads they think will appear during the show. Give one point for each category answer and an additional point if they guess the company that placed the ad. Plan on seven or eight commercials an hour.

Exchange papers before the show and have each player give reasons for their selections. After the show, award a small prize to the viewer with the highest score.

Example: If the show was a basketball game

CATEGORY	BRAND
Sport Shoes	Nike
Beer	Bud
Cars	Chevrolet

Ask your family why they think these types of commercials appear on this particular show?

Media Skill Builder: Break the Bank

As your family watches TV, have a paper and pencil and write down the approximate cost of each item that is advertised. At the end of each program, total the amount you would have spent if you had purchased every item. Discuss with your children what the advertiser is trying to do. Note: Starting wage at a McDonald's Restaurant is between $4.65 and $5.00 an hour.

Media Skill Builder: Commercial Investigator

Purpose: To make families aware of gimmicks sponsors use to make us want to buy their products. (Older children might research food photography or special effects.)

Copy the following list on a piece of paper or duplicate the page. As viewers watch commercials, have them answer the questions. Discuss the results.

How many times does the name or trademark of the product appear? _____times   Why?

Does the product appear larger or stronger than it does in real life? _____YES ____NO

If it is a food item, is it as fresh and delicious when served as it is presented in the commercial?   _____YES _____NO

Is the product presented in a realistic setting? _____YES ____NO

Is the setting exceptionally beautiful or glamorous? _____YES ____NO

Do the music and sound effects attract you to the product? _____YES ____NO

Are the scenes presenting the product extremely romantic or funny?
_____YES _____NO

Does the product perform as well in person as it does in the ads?
_____YES _____NO

• **What About the Unexpected and Violence?**

Child experts tell parents to monitor their children's viewing and talk to them about what they see on TV. Of course, the experts aren't sitting in the family room during prime time watching a family show when an ad for the late night flick flashes on the screen. Before you can grab the remote control, a woman clutching her fur coat around her throat, throws her arms open and casts the coat aside. There she stands center screen in her bikini underwear and high heels for two seconds, then — flash, she's gone. And you're supposed to talk to the kids.

One of the best things you can do in this situation is talk back to the TV. This approach has four advantages: 1) you can't offend the TV; 2) you're not lecturing to your children; 3) kids love to eavesdrop on conversations; and 4) your kids learn what you think. If you remain awkwardly silent, your children may interpret your silence as approval of what's been shown. You can also talk back if you think shows are biased, presenting opinions as facts, or leaving out important information. Best of all, you'll create an experience your children will remember.

Have you ever selected a show for the family to watch and it becomes suddenly violent? The family doesn't want to turn it off; what can you do? Mr. Rogers suggests asking the child to "look for the helpers" — the characters in the program who are aiding the victim, seeking justice, or just doing the morally right thing.[58] This helps the child view the show from a different perspective.

These strategies for dealing with the unexpected do not replace family discussions and explanations. As we've mentioned if children are to become media smart, parents have to talk with them, not at them, about what's on the screen.

Fast-paced action holds viewers' attention. Both physical and verbal violence incorporates action into shows and cartoons. If a family turns on the TV, chances are their children will be exposed to some form of violence. What's a parent to say?

Begin by discussing the differences between an actor and a character. An actor is a person whose job it is to make us believe he is someone else. To create this illusion he/she uses make-up, costumes and props. The person the actor portrays is called a character. Some characters are make-believe like Alf or Star Trek's Spock. Some are dramatized persons from historic events like Abraham Lincoln in "The Civil War" series.

Whether a show about make believe or a dramatization of history, when violence appears on the screen, special effects have been used to create that illusion. Emphasize that the actors practice appearing to fight but don't really hurt each other. The sound, special props (like chairs that break easily), and other special effects make the audience believe they are witnessing a fight. If children learn to wonder, "How did they do that"? during violent scenes, they will be less involved with the violence itself.

Media Skill Building: Violent Action Awareness

As the family watches an action packed cartoon or show, note the violent actions.

Show Name _____

_____How many characters are injured?

_____How many characters die violently?

There was a fire.   _____YES _____NO

There were car chases.   _____YES _____NO

There were car accidents.   _____YES _____NO

Could the violence have been avoided? How?

Another type of violence is the verbal assault. Caustic comments of a comic "put-down" overlaid with laugh-tracks may appear funny to a child. In reality, few people like being on the receiving end of such an assault. Parents can point out that in real life these words should not be used because they can hurt people's feelings. Have the child notice the person being laughed at is usually the person spouting the words, not the victim.

86

*The Television
Planning System*

There were _____ "put downs" in the show.

The "put downs" attacked the person's:

      appearance

      character

      habits

      nationality

      race

      gender

      abilities

What caused the attack?

Did it change anything? How?

The violent, quick-fix solution to disagreements can be debunked if parents talk with their children.

• The Power Struggle

TV influences all of us. Some of the most creative minds in the world labor to make it informative, believable, and entertaining. It's power emanates from the influence it exerts on our thinking and therefore our behavior.

The creators of TV programs help shape our future culture. Their programs place in the minds of children the writers' vision of today's world. As children mature, some of these visions will be the building blocks for their values. Some TV creators assume their role of cultural vanguard with responsible concern. Others feel no accountability for the future they are instrumental in creating.

Societal debates about the content of TV fare are as old as the medium, one side denouncing censorship, the other side calling for social responsiibility. While the struggle continues, little boys and girls grow into men and women.

Parents cannot expect this ageless struggle to be resolved, freeing them of their concerns. The hope for our children and culture is that parents gain a more realistic view of the total impact TV has on the minds and bodies of their children and assume their role as guardians.

The power struggle that surrounds TV is not between parents and children: the parent wanting the children to limit their viewing and the children wanting to do what they want. The struggle is between the parent and the TV — which will control the molding of the developing child's mind and body? TVPS helps families make peace with TV.

When parents guide their children through the decision making process and encourage them be selective TV viewers, they prepare their children to make decisions in the future. Teaching children to question what they see and hear on TV helps young people to become thinking adults. By limiting children to what families decide is the best of TV, parents enrich their children's lives.

HELPS TO PUT AWAY THE TV

The following devices are listed from the least to the most expensive.

- **The Switch**

  The Switch is a mechanical device that regulates the flow of electricity to the TV with a key. The TV's plug is captured in a child-proof compartment so children cannot reconnect the TV. When the family decides to view TV, they turn the key of The Switch "on," leaving The Switch "off" at other times. With The Switch off, the TV cannot be turned on, video games and video tapes cannot be viewed. However, families can still record programs on their VCR.

THE SWITCH, Model TS 100A

Price: $24 post-paid. For information about THE SWITCH, Model TS100A,
contact THE SWITCH,
P.O. Box 344, Western Springs, IL 60558, call 800-535-5845

*Helps to Put Away
The TV*

• Super*Vision*

SuperVision allows families to program their children's TV viewing times. SuperVision can turn the TV on and off for two different time periods of any length per day. Two time periods can be set for each day for four different children. The time periods can vary from day to day during a given week to accommodate the child's favorite programs.

SuperVision also tabulates the amount of time a specific child has the TV on and adds it to a running total for the day and week. This allows families to set and monitor each child's daily and weekly TV allowance. Parents can override the system with their password. The display on the unit leads parents through the programming process.

SUPER*VISION*

Price: around $100.00. For information about SuperVision, contact Tectrics Labs, Inc., 5256 South Mission Road, Suite 110, Bonsall, CA 92003 or call 800- 845-1911.

*Helps to Put Away
The TV*

Helps to Put Away The TV

• Time*Slot*

TimeSlot hopefully will enter the market in 1992. It also fastens to the power cord. Using an administrator card, parents program the number of hours of TV "credit" each child shall have. To activate the TV, the child must enter his programmed card into the TimeSlot reader. As long as the TV is on, time is deducted from the card. A display on the TimeSlot unit advises how much time remains on the card. When the time is up, the card no longer turns the TV set on until it is reprogrammed by a parent.

With the administrator card, parents can override the program or audit the amount of time left in the child's account.

TIME*SLOT*

Price: around $100. For information contact
Design Dimension Inc.,
901 North West Street, Raleigh, NC 27603, or call 919-828-1485.

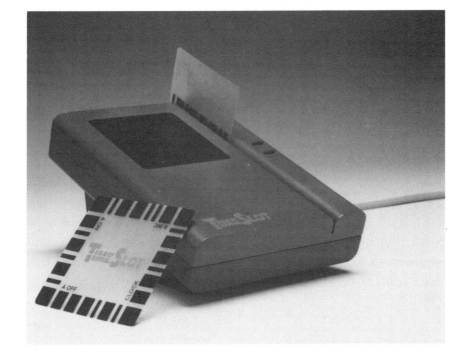

A P P E N D I X I I

96

TV PLANNING SYSTEM (TVPS) RECORD

The following pages contain forms for TV planning. Make copies of the forms if you wish to continue using TVPS.

Fill in dates for the week and set a Goal for Week's Total Tube Time (TV, video tapes and game times) for the week. With the help of a TV program guide, select the programs the family wishes to watch and write them and their times on the TVPS Daily Record. Try to include the entire family in making these decisions. At the end of the week, total the time spent in front of the tube each day, enter the totals on the weekly record and compute. Compare the Actual Total Tube Time with the week's Goal. Evaluate. If you meet your Goal, celebrate!

TVPS WEEK'S RECORD

Week of _____ to _____

Goal for the week's total tube time is _____ hours _____ min.

Sunday's total _____ hrs. _____ min.

Monday's total _____ hrs. _____ min.

Tuesday's total _____ hrs. _____ min.

Wednesday's total _____ hrs. _____ min.

Thursday's total _____ hrs. _____ min.

Friday's total _____ hrs. _____ min.

Saturday's total _____ hrs. _____ min.

ACTUAL TOTAL TUBE TIME _____ hours _____ min.

97

*TV Planning System
(TVPS) Record*

TVPS DAILY RECORD

Sunday's Record

*TV Planning System
(TVPS) Record*

TV Program or Video	Beginning Time	Ending Time	Total Show Time
_____			
_____			
_____			
_____			
_____			

Video Game Time_____

Sunday's Total Tube Time_____hrs._____min.

TVPS DAILY RECORD

Monday's Record

TV Program or Video	Beginning Time	Ending Time	Total Show Time

TV Planning System (TVPS) Record

Video Game Time _____

Monday's Total Tube Time_____hrs._____min.

TVPS DAILY RECORD

100

*TV Planning System
(TVPS) Record*

Tuesday's Record

TV Program or Video	Beginning Time	Ending Time	Total Show Time
_____	_____	_____	_____
_____	_____	_____	_____
_____	_____	_____	_____
_____	_____	_____	_____
_____	_____	_____	_____

Video Game Time _____

Tuesday's Total Tube Time _____ hrs. _____ min.

TVPS DAILY RECORD

Wednesday's Record

TV Program or Video	Beginning Time	Ending Time	Total Show Time

TV Planning System (TVPS) Record

Video Game Time_____

Wednesday's Total Tube Time_____hrs._____min.

TVPS DAILY RECORD

| 102 | **Thursday's Record** |

*TV Planning System
(TVPS) Record*

TV Program or Video	Beginning Time	Ending Time	Total Show Time

Video Game Time _____

Thursday's Total Tube Time_____hrs._____min.

TVPS DAILY RECORD

Friday's Record

TV Program or Video	Beginning Time	Ending Time	Total Show Time

TV Planning System (TVPS) Record

_____

_____

_____

_____

_____

Video Game Time_____

Friday's Total Tube Time_____hrs._____min.

TVPS DAILY RECORD

Saturday's Record

TV Program or Video	Beginning Time	Ending Time	Total Show Time
_____	_____	_____	_____
_____	_____	_____	_____
_____	_____	_____	_____
_____	_____	_____	_____
_____	_____	_____	_____

Video Game Time_____

Saturday's Total Tube Time_____hrs._____min.

TVPS WEEK'S RECORD

Week of _____ to _____

*TV Planning System
(TVPS) Record*

Goal for the week's total tube time is _____ hours _____ min.

Sunday's total _____ hrs. _____ min.

Monday's total _____ hrs. _____ min.

Tuesday's total _____ hrs. _____ min.

Wednesday's total _____ hrs. _____ min.

Thursday's total _____ hrs. _____ min.

Friday's total _____ hrs. _____ min.

Saturday's total _____ hrs. _____ min.

ACTUAL TOTAL TUBE TIME _____ hours _____ min.

TVPS DAILY RECORD

TV Planning System (TVPS) Record

Sunday's Record

TV Program or Video	Beginning Time	Ending Time	Total Show Time
_____	_____	_____	_____
_____	_____	_____	_____
_____	_____	_____	_____
_____	_____	_____	_____
_____	_____	_____	_____

Video Game Time_____

Sunday's Total Tube Time_____hrs._____min.

TVPS DAILY RECORD

Monday's Record

TV Program or Video	Beginning Time	Ending Time	Total Show Time

TV Planning System (TVPS) Record

Video Game Time_____

Monday's Total Tube Time_____hrs._____min.

TVPS DAILY RECORD

108

TV Planning System (TVPS) Record

Tuesday's Record

TV Program or Video	Beginning Time	Ending Time	Total Show Time

Video Game Time_____

Tuesday's Total Tube Time_____hrs._____min.

TVPS DAILY RECORD

Wednesday's Record

TV Program or Video	Beginning Time	Ending Time	Total Show Time

TV Planning System (TVPS) Record

Video Game Time _____

Wednesday's Total Tube Time_____hrs._____min.

TVPS DAILY RECORD

*TV Planning System
(TVPS) Record*

Thursday's Record

TV Program or Video	Beginning Time	Ending Time	Total Show Time
_____			
_____			
_____			
_____			
_____			

Video Game Time _____

Thursday's Total Tube Time _____ hrs. _____ min.

TVPS DAILY RECORD

Friday's Record

TV Program or Video	Beginning Time	Ending Time	Total Show Time	*TV Planning System (TVPS) Record*

Video Game Time_____

Friday's Total Tube Time_____hrs._____min.

TVPS DAILY RECORD

112

Saturday's Record

TV Planning System (TVPS) Record

TV Program or Video	Beginning Time	Ending Time	Total Show Time

Video Game Time_____

Saturday's Total Tube Time_____hrs._____min.

TVPS WEEK'S RECORD

Week of _____to_____

*TV Planning System
(TVPS) Record*

Goal for the week's total tube time is _____hours _____min.

Sunday's total _____hrs. _____ min.

Monday's total _____hrs. _____ min.

Tuesday's total _____hrs. _____ min.

Wednesday's total _____hrs. _____ min.

Thursday's total _____hrs. _____ min.

Friday's total _____hrs. _____ min.

Saturday's total _____hrs. _____ min.

ACTUAL TOTAL TUBE TIME _____hours_____min.

TVPS DAILY RECORD

Sunday's Record

*TV Planning System
(TVPS) Record*

TV Program or Video	Beginning Time	Ending Time	Total Show Time
_____	_____	_____	_____
_____	_____	_____	_____
_____	_____	_____	_____
_____	_____	_____	_____
_____	_____	_____	_____

Video Game Time_____

Sunday's Total Tube Time_____hrs._____min.

TVPS DAILY RECORD

Monday's Record

TV Program or Video	Beginning Time	Ending Time	Total Show Time

TV Planning System (TVPS) Record

_____

_____

_____

_____

_____

Video Game Time _____

Monday's Total Tube Time _____ hrs. _____ min.

TVPS DAILY RECORD

116

Tuesday's Record

TV Program or Video	Beginning Time	Ending Time	Total Show Time

Video Game Time _____

Tuesday's Total Tube Time_____hrs._____min.

TVPS DAILY RECORD

Wednesday's Record

TV Program or Video	Beginning Time	Ending Time	Total Show Time

TV Planning System (TVPS) Record

Video Game Time_____

Wednesday's Total Tube Time_____hrs._____min.

TVPS DAILY RECORD

118

Thursday's Record

TV Planning System (TVPS) Record

TV Program or Video	Beginning Time	Ending Time	Total Show Time

Video Game Time _____

Thursday's Total Tube Time _____ hrs. _____ min.

TVPS DAILY RECORD

Friday's Record

TV Program or Video	Beginning Time	Ending Time	Total Show Time
___			
___			
___			
___			
___			

TV Planning System (TVPS) Record

Video Game Time _____

Friday's Total Tube Time _____ hrs. _____ min.

TVPS DAILY RECORD

| 120 | **Saturday's Record** |

TV Planning System (TVPS) Record

TV Program or Video	Beginning Time	Ending Time	Total Show Time
_____	_____	_____	_____
_____	_____	_____	_____
_____	_____	_____	_____
_____	_____	_____	_____
_____	_____	_____	_____

Video Game Time _____

Saturday's Total Tube Time _____ hrs. _____ min.

TVPS WEEK'S RECORD

Week of _____ to _____

Goal for the week's total tube time is _____ hours _____ min.

Sunday's total _____ hrs. _____ min.

Monday's total _____ hrs. _____ min.

Tuesday's total _____ hrs. _____ min.

Wednesday's total _____ hrs. _____ min.

Thursday's total _____ hrs. _____ min.

Friday's total _____ hrs. _____ min.

Saturday's total _____ hrs. _____ min.

ACTUAL TOTAL TUBE TIME _____ hours _____ min.

*TV Planning System
(TVPS) Record*

TVPS DAILY RECORD

122

Sunday's Record

TV Planning System (TVPS) Record

TV Program or Video	Beginning Time	Ending Time	Total Show Time
_____			
_____			
_____			
_____			
_____			

Video Game Time_____

Sunday's Total Tube Time_____hrs._____min.

TVPS DAILY RECORD

Monday's Record

TV Program or Video	Beginning Time	Ending Time	Total Show Time

TV Planning System (TVPS) Record

_____

_____

_____

_____

_____

Video Game Time_____

Monday's Total Tube Time_____hrs._____min.

TVPS DAILY RECORD

124

Tuesday's Record

*TV Planning System
(TVPS) Record*

TV Program or Video	Beginning Time	Ending Time	Total Show Time
_____			
_____			
_____			
_____			
_____			

Video Game Time _____

Tuesday's Total Tube Time_____hrs._____min.

TVPS DAILY RECORD

Wednesday's Record

TV Program or Video	Beginning Time	Ending Time	Total Show Time

TV Planning System (TVPS) Record

_____

_____

_____

_____

_____

Video Game Time _____

Wednesday's Total Tube Time_____hrs._____min.

TVPS DAILY RECORD

126

Thursday's Record

*TV Planning System
(TVPS) Record*

TV Program or Video	Beginning Time	Ending Time	Total Show Time

Video Game Time _____

Thursday's Total Tube Time_____hrs._____min.

TVPS DAILY RECORD

Friday's Record

TV Program or Video	Beginning Time	Ending Time	Total Show Time

TV Planning System (TVPS) Record

Video Game Time _____

Friday's Total Tube Time_____hrs._____min.

TVPS DAILY RECORD

Saturday's Record

*TV Planning System
(TVPS) Record*

TV Program or Video	Beginning Time	Ending Time	Total Show Time

Video Game Time_____

Saturday's Total Tube Time_____hrs._____min.

REFERENCES

1. "American Academy of Pediatrics Policy Statement Update," *AAPNews*, April 1990.
2. Robert Kubey and Mihaly Csikzentmihalyi, *Television and The Quality of Life: How Viewing Shapes Everyday Experience*, Lawrence Erlbaum Associates, Publishers, Hillsdale, NJ, 1990, p. xi.
3. Same as 1.
4. Marian, Burros, "Obese kids are a growing problem in high fat society," *Chicago Tribune*, January 18, 1990, Section 7, p. 9.
5. Jon Van, "Cholesterol high in kids glued to TV," *Chicago Tribune*, November 14, 1990, Sec. 1, p. 3.
6. Same as 5.
7. "Boot camp gets softer for couch potatoes," *Chicago Tribune*, April 17, 1990, p. 1.
8. Bob Tita, "Youths spend less time at physical activity," *Reporter/Progress Newspapers*, March 16-17, 1989, p. 8.
9. Eileen Ogintz, "Winning by losing," *Chicago Tribune*, October 12, 1990, Section 5, pp. 1-2.
10. "Verbal scores on SAT sink to a 10-year low," *Chicago Tribune*, August 28, 1990, p.1.
11. Linda Ellerbee, *MOVE ON: Adventures in the Real World*, C.P. Putnam's Sons, NY, 1991, p.18.

12. Ellerbee, Same as 11, p. 31.
13. Ellerbee, Same as 11, p. 26 and p. 29.
14. Kubey, Same as 2, p. 135.
15. Kubey, Same as 2, p. 190.
16. Jon Van, "TV viewing linked to childhood obesity, violence," *Chicago Tribune*, April 17, 1990, p. 1.
17. Kubey, Same as 2, p. 168.
18. "Spoils of a good air war," *US News and World Report,* Sept. 10, 1990, p. 76.
19. Bank Street College, William H. Hooks, editor, *The Pleasure of Their Company: How To Have More Fun With Your Children*, Chilton Book Company, Radnor, PA, 1981, p. 79.
20. "Cowabunga, mate," *Chicago Tribune*, July 23, 1990, Section 1, p. 12.
21. "Parental Guidance Suggested," *The Cable Guide*, October 1990, p. 42.
22. Ira Wolfman, "Is TV programming Your Family? Cosby VS. The Simpsons," *Family Circle*, October 16, 1990, p. 79.
23. Mike Royko, "Turn off the TV, tune in the kids," *Chicago Tribune*, April 25, 1990, Sec. 1, p. 3.
24. *Television and The Family*, The American Academy of Pediatrics, Elk Grove Village, IL, May 1986.
25. Dr. James Dobson and Gary L Bauer, *Children At Risk: The Battle for the Hearts and Minds of Our Children*, Word Publishing, Dallas, TX, 1990, p. 206.

26. Joan Beck, *Effective Parenting*, Simon & Schusster, NY, 1976, p. 220.

27. AAP, 1990, Same as 1.

28. Balter, Dr. Lawrence, *Who's In Control: Dr. Balter's Guide to Discipline Without Combat*, Posidon Press, NY, 1988, p. 130.

29. Wolfman, Same as 22.

30. Dobson, Same as 25, p. 208.

31. Fred Rogers, "What Kids Should Believe About Make-Believe," *The Cable Guide*, October 1990, p. 44.

32. "Parental Guidance Suggested: How to Help Your Kids Use TV Wisely," *The Cable Guide*, October 1990, p. 42.

33. Benjamin Spock, M.D. and Michael Rothenberg, M.D., *Dr. Spock's Baby and Child Care*, Pocket Books, NY p. 475.

34. Gene I. Maeroff, *The School-Smart Parent: A guide to knowing what your child should know — from infancy through elementary school*, Time Books, New York, NY, 1989, p. 119.

35. Bank Street College, Same as 19.

36. Herbert London, "What TV Drama Is Teaching Our Children," *The New York Times*, August 23, 1987, Page 23.

37. London, Same as 36.

38. Fred Rogers, *Mister Rogers Talks With Parents*, Berkley Books, NY, 1983, p. 184.

39. Dorothy and Jerome Singer, *The Parent's Guide: Use TV to your Child's Advantage*, Acropolis Books Ltd., Reston, VA, 1990, p. 32.

40. Marianne Neifert, M.D., *Dr. Mom: A Guide to Baby and Child Care*, G. P.Putnam's Son, New York, NY, 1986, p. 344.
41. Glenn Austin, M.D., *Love & Power: Parent & Child*, Robert Erdmann Publishing, San Marcos, CA, 1988, p. 93.
42. Peter Williamson, Ph.D., *Good Kids, Bad Behavior: Helping Children Learn Self Discipline*, Simon & Schuster, NY, 1990, p. 99.
43. Peter Williamson, "Holding The Line," *PARENTING*, May 1990, p. 90.
44. Williamson, Ph.D., Same as 42, p. 92.
45. Lisa Anderson, "Boredom: It's no yawning matter," *Chicago Tribune*, July 15, 1991, Sec. 5, p. 5.
46. Anderson, Same as 45, p. 5.
47. Kubey, Same as 2, p. 200.
48. Marie Winn, *The "No TV Week" Guide: Unplugging The Plug-In Drug*, Penguin Books, NY, 1987, p. 155.
49. Winn, Same as 48, p. 157.
50. Winn, Same as 48, p. 157.
51. Kubey, Same as 2, p. 191.
52. Gene Bylinsky, "The Marvels of 'Virtual Reality,'" *FORTUNE*, June 3, 1991, p. 138 & 150.
53. Bylinsky, Same as 52, p. 142.
54. Thomas Toch, "Wired for learning," *US News and World Report*, October 28, 1991, p. 77.

55. Harvey S. Wiener, *Talk With Your Children: How to develop reading and language skills through conversation at home*, Viking Books, New York, NY, 1988 p. 191.
56. "That was the year that was, on TV," *Chicago Tribune*, January 2, 1992, Section 1, p. 24.
57. John Condry, *The Psychology of Television*, Lawrence Erlbaum Associates, Publishers, Hillsdale, NJ, 1989, p. 29.
58. Same as 57, p. 23.
59. Rogers, Same as 38, p. 183.

Other Helpful Sources

Bennett, Steve and Ruth, *365 TV - Free Activities*, Bob Adams Publishing— order by calling 800-872-5627.
Center for Media and Values; 1962 South Shenandoah, Los Angeles, CA 90034, (They publish a magazine called Media and Values and can provide a variety of materials relating to the media.)
Cutright, Melitta J., Ph.D.,*The National PTA Talks to Parents,* Doubleday, NY, 1989.
De Franco, Ellen B., "How to Be A Smart TV Watcher: A Special Pull-out Page for Kids!, *Media & Values*, p. 29, Fall 1990/Winter 1991.

Kuczen, Barbara, Ph.D., *Childhood Stress: Don't Let Your Child Be A Victim,* Delacorte Press, NY, 1982.

Miller, Gordon Porter, *Teaching Your Child To Make Decision: How To Raise A Responsible Child,* Harper & Row, Publishers, NY, 1984.

Singer, Dorthy and Jerome, Ph.D., *Use TV To Your Child's Advantage,* Acropolis Press, 1990.

INDEX